GEORG EISLER **FROM**

NAKED
TO NUDE

LIFE DRAWING IN THE
TWENTIETH CENTURY

WITH 91 ILLUSTRATIONS   8 IN COLOR

WILLIAM MORROW AND CO.,INC.

7.?.~0

Library of Congress Catalog Card Number 76-47085

ISBN 0-688-08167-3 (pbk.)

Preface

I believe that drawing can be taught and learnt – that it is a method of communication, and complete indifference to it is the exception rather than the rule. This assumption is based on a certain experience on my part, as a student, as an artist, and as a teacher of life-drawing, which is the most concrete form of learning to see and draw. The human body is in many ways the ideal study-object for the draughtsman. It is immediately identifiable, there is a wealth of works to study, ranging through all periods of art, and it is a fascinating subject in itself.

Life-drawing should not be restricted to the artist and the art-student. There are many possibilities also for the amateur; numerous art-clubs and adult education schemes have included life-classes in their programmes.

It is of course frequently argued that creativity cannot be taught, that it is a spontaneous urge, limited to those with special talent. This is true to a certain extent, but should not serve to isolate the artist as a sacred cow of society, an object of idolization by a few connoisseurs able to purchase his work and of indifference to the great majority. Through drawing from nature we are all able to observe and follow, and also to participate in, one of the fundamental creative aspects of visual art, which need never be the privilege of the happy few. This knowledge increases the enjoyment of all art.

I have studied life-drawing under a number of teachers, starting in art-schools in Great Britain during the latter half of the Second World War. In the early 1940s the ideal of the life-classes of the English art schools was Augustus John, whom we regarded with awe as a twentieth-century reincarnation of the Renaissance masters. Before we were allowed into the life-class a lot of time and effort had to be spent in drawing from plaster casts of antique sculpture, of which great numbers were gathering dust in the art-schools. Drawing was considered a matter of strict discipline, great attention being paid to exact proportion, correct shading and degree of finish. Looking back, I think with a certain gratitude of the stern disciplinarians who taught me the meaning of hard work, the use of the pencil and, most important, of the eraser, as well as a strict sense of proportion.

Later in Vienna I was fortunate to attend for many years Herbert Boeckl's life-class at the Academy of Fine Arts. This important painter at that time limited his teaching to life-drawing. It was not only the ever-present example of his own magnificent work in that field which filled the class, but also his most individual approach to posing, and to the use of artificial light, and his terse and pungent comments on our efforts. Occasionally he would sit and draw with his students, and we could observe the laborious and painstaking evolution of a leg, a breast or a knee on a white square of paper. Of his many dicta on life-drawing I cannot resist quoting one: 'Draw the feet, draw the hands – the rest is easy.'

Ranuccio Bianchi Bandinelli, the eminent scholar of Etruscan and Roman art, many years ago first drew my attention to the significance of the depiction of the naked body as a vessel of ideas and thoughts in European art. In many subsequent talks I was able to learn much about the interplay of art, society and history.

To the memory of both these exceptional men, the artist and the art-historian, this book is dedicated.

Introduction

We have schooled ourselves to see by acquiring the capacity to depict ourselves. The study of the human body – one of the chief pre-occupations of the Renaissance artist – enhanced more than the plastic arts. The ability to portray man also led to the development of modern medicine: as it became increasingly possible to record the structure of the human body in a lifelike way, the study of anatomy ceased to be mystical guesswork. Drawing is one of the most important forms of communication: the engineer, the designer, the architect, the statistician, all bear out the Chinese proverb that 'a picture is worth a thousand words'. This book is devoted to drawing as an extended method of seeing and of recording experience – seen through its concentration on the human body as our most personal self.

Our attitude towards the body has undergone many changes since the Renaissance. Though much of the mystery has gone, a certain mystique remains. Over-exposure to nakedness (hardly an aspect of advertising seems to be able to do without it) has apparently failed to blunt the senses entirely. From the private pleasure of depicting the patron-king's mistress to the business of generating sales through a sex-symbol multiplied infinitely, the image of the naked body has remained a significant fetish. There is, however, a great difference between the naked and the nude in art. Kenneth Clark has given a concise definition: 'The nude is not the subject of art but a form of art.'

A group of sculpture-students at the Academy of Florence were so enchanted by a very young and beautifully proportioned model that they made a plaster cast from her body, expecting a perfect replica of the girl. The result was, in the words of one of the participants, 'a hideous cadaver'. The subject had not become an artistic form: the naked had not undergone that transformation necessary to the nude. It is exactly this quality which lends to the painted casts in polyester of the new Hyper-Realists their character of horrifying alienation. These figures are not interpretations, and in the process of reproduction all the sensuality inherent in living flesh disappears. Through the most easily identifiable subject of art in the world, the human body, we learn to read the language of draughtsmanship, to see with the artist's eyes, to follow the line, the moulding of form on a flat square of paper, as well as the ever-surprising transition to the three-dimensional. The tactile quality of a good drawing or painting sets it apart from the pseudo-perfection of mechanical reproduction.

For centuries, drawing from the nude was almost exclusively confined to life-classes in the academies and was considered first and foremost a subject of practical importance. It was clearly established that it was difficult to depict the clothed figure without knowledge of the body underneath. There was – and is – something clinically impersonal about a life-class: after shedding his or her clothes behind a screen, the model takes up a pose determined by the teacher and remains still in the neutral surroundings of a large room.

In the nineteenth century the nude became less an object for preparatory study than a subject in its own right. Nudes had of course featured prominently in paintings and graphics of all periods and styles, but with few exceptions (such as Rembrandt's) they had been placed in appropriate settings and narrative contexts. Susannah and the Elders, the Bath of Diana, Bathsheba, the Judgment of Paris and other biblical or mythological themes had been ideal *raisons d'être*. Artists now started to dispense with these themes, and the nude was increasingly emancipated as its own subject matter. The last universal and international art-style, Neoclassicism, disintegrated, and the polarization of art between academicism and the avant-garde took its place. It was in the studios, usually located in the top storey of the tenements of big cities (they, too, were an innovation of the nineteenth century), that the non-Establishment artist assumed his new-found role on the fringe of society. The subject matter of his work became increasingly personal and was produced for an often desperately small market of friends and occasional patrons. The grand mythological and religious theatre of preceding periods lived on in a much commercialized and diluted form in the salons and academies, which included a repertoire of pretexts for the display of unclothed female bodies, the slave-market and other scenes of classical antiquity being popular themes. In opposition to this was the artist as an outsider, and the act of painting became its own subject in the work of the founding fathers of modern art.

In this milieu arose the new romanticism of *la vie de Bohème*, the cult of the artist living in direct contradiction to smug respectability, flouting the values of the overfurnished, overdressed and overfed bourgeoisie. Nakedness was an important factor in the issue, the naked model in the studio being the object of secret envy and fascination. In a society where the glimpse of an uncovered female leg even below the knee was considered greatly immodest, and everyday dress sought to hide the natural forms of the female body, the depicting of the naked female in art – even academic art – assumed a sociological significance.

It is undeniable that, in drawing and painting, the female body is much more frequently dealt with than the male. This is not only to be explained by the obvious fact that the unclothed woman is usually far more attractive to the artist (up to the present day, the majority of artists and collectors of art have been men). It is also true that the female body offers a greater variety of forms and contours to draw, and light and shadow have more differentiated forms and surfaces to define. This does not of course rule out the motive of sexual interest on the part of the artist, as well as on that of the viewer, in a dominantly masculine society.

In bourgeois society the coquetry emanating from the nude is not directed only at an 'owner-viewer' (as John Berger calls the male watcher for whom erotic nudes are painted); there is another side to the coin. Sexuality has been woman's only weapon; and as the *femme fatale* she gains dominion over her patron. The viewer is reduced to a *voyeur*. In Courbet we find her for the first time living a sexuality all her own, which is an enormous sociological step. His *Sleepers* unashamedly expose their splendid bodies for their very own enjoyment; their amorous play has clearly given them intense pleasure, and their attention is wholly devoted to each other without coquetry directed beyond the painting at the viewer.

In the nineteenth century life drawing and life painting became more and more a part of everyday studio activity, sometimes becoming the object of intense emotional involvement. (Delacroix in his diary: 'I saw Sidonia last Tuesday. What ravishing moments! How lovely she looked lying naked on the bed!') Often artists had many models in constant attendance: in the studios of Rodin and Klimt, there was something of an hour-by-hour duty-roster; Degas, with the bath-tub as an important part of his studio-furniture, worked in direct contradiction to classical or romantic poses, observing women in their usually unobserved moments, as when getting in and out of the bath, washing or drying themselves, thus rendering sensuality in everyday occurrences.

5

The spectacular erotic display was superseded by a more differentiated and in many respects a more sober approach. Picasso's historic *Demoiselles d'Avignon* depicts a brothel scene, which was, thematically at least, not far removed from the subject matter of Degas or Toulouse-Lautrec, who in their turn had taken the motive of Ingres' *Turkish Bath* (merely a somewhat overcrowded if idealized brothel under another name) a step further. But the Cubists were to use the nude in an unashamedly non-erotic manner, reducing it to the function of the module and thereby gaining a formal, non-associative basis for their excursions into new aspects of three-dimensionality.

With Central-European Expressionism a new approach to the nude was made manifest. Its roots lay not only in the German Renaissance, but above all in the new programme of the Expressionists, reflected in their style, in which perception is always strongly coloured by emotion. The appearance of a new catalogue of subject matter brought with it a number of new stylistic possibilities. This is especially found in the diversity of the treatment of the naked human body in twentieth-century art.

The often frightening mechanization and specialization of our present-day society has done more than put an end to any homogeneous view of the world: the fragmentation of traditional patterns has found its reflection in art. 'Is not style the most unequivocal expression of a society?' asks Ernst Fischer.

In Nazi art nakedness had a special role to fulfil: unclothed man, as the idealized warrior displaying muscles and aggressiveness, or sweating healthily after a hard day's toil, and woman with well-rounded hips and breasts for breeding new generations of equally perfect specimens. Italian Fascism was more concerned with neo-Roman poses, with or without toga. At the other end of the political scale, Socialist Realism, with its pseudo-proletarian puritanism, long focused its interest on the body-building rewards of hard work for the good of the state, women being invariably clothed.

Commercialization of sensual experience, thanks to the mass-media, has been responsible for the reduction of sexual imagery from an expensive commodity to a sort of small-change of throw-away porn in handy packages. It has brought with it a massive standardization and the emergence of the universal sex-symbol against which reality must inevitably compete. This synthetic ideal undergoes various marked changes in a relatively short time, from big-busted and round-hipped to slender with diminutive forms and back again. In its ever-shortening tenure, it nevertheless exerts a rigorous dictatorship. Inevitably these norms find their way into art, whether as accepted values or as objects of criticism, sometimes of caricature, sometimes as a stimulus to pursue the opposite extreme, The drawings in this book show how, as a consequence, the subject of the nude in twentieth-century art undergoes constant and significant changes, reflecting the increasingly problematic role of the artist in contemporary society.

Anatomy

'This arm is so beautifully painted, it can't be long enough,' replied the German painter Max Liebermann to a critic who had considered the arm of Cézanne's *Portrait of a Boy* too long.

Since Antiquity the search for the exact proportions of the human body has obsessed many great artists. It was maintained that the ideal body might be reduced to a certain quasi-geometrical formula. Vitruvius, in the first century BC, established a system of measurement of the human body: a man lying on the floor with arms and legs spread could be contained perfectly within a square. In the Renaissance, Leonardo and other artists, including Albrecht Dürer, took up this scheme, which was based on measurement of antique sculptures. Vitruvius also gave a number of basic proportions. For example, the face is one-tenth of the overall length of the body, the head one-eighth, the foot one-sixth, the distance between fingertip and elbow one-quarter, as is the width of the chest. The face is divided into three equal parts: forehead, nose and the distance between nose and chin.

Leon Battista Alberti (c. 1404–72) worked in measurements of 'feet', dividing the body into six lengths of one 'foot', each 'foot' consisting of ten divisions which in turn were subdivided by ten; all these proportions were arrived at by measuring living models. On this basis he established an aesthetic norm as a method of determining physical beauty – a form of balance between the typical and the ideal.

In subsequent periods artists came to rely more and more on these measurements, imposing their norms on nature. Dürer in his *Four Books of Human Proportions* (published 1528) first adapted these measurements to the female body. His lasting contribution, however, was to include various physical types, previously rejected as ugly and deformed, into his system of proportion. In this rejection of the ideal he was a remarkably modern artist.

A more or less sound schooling in anatomy used to be the rule in most academies and art-schools, and has only recently gone out of fashion. At the Vienna Academy in the post-war years the teaching of anatomy was still in the hands of a brilliant and thorough *Prosektor*, Professor Paul. This professor issued from his usual haunt, the Franz-Joseph Hospital, frequently bearing grisly specimens which he then proceeded to dissect in the life-class. These practical demonstrations were fascinating and eminently useful to those of his students who had strong enough stomachs to watch them.

My own teacher Herbert Boeckl spent long hours in the dissecting-theatre, working on his horrifyingly beautiful drawings of corpses. Even if the majority of his students were not prepared to follow him there, the life-class of the Vienna Academy was pervaded by the knowledge of what went on beneath the surface of the body: which muscles and bones determined movement and the distribution of weight. Such an awareness distinguishes all significant life-drawings. This does not imply that all artists have to be anatomists in order to draw the nude, but rather that at some point they should at least be interested in the subject.

Even with the greatest departure from naturalistic depiction a basis of anatomical information is of great use, for it is always good to know what we are ruling out. It is not the purpose of life-drawing to copy nature slavishly, an idea against which Delacroix warned over a hundred years ago. A knowledge of the structure of the human body nevertheless enables us to abstract from nature with greater freedom.

The majority of the works brought together in this book must not be regarded as in any way an exact representation of anatomy or proportion. But even in those instances where the artist has been most free in his use of distortion or invention, we always find a sense of physical presence, of functional logic. However synthetic these figures may be, they are based on a system of measurements and proportions, sometimes intuitive, sometimes (as in Cubism) worked out schematically.

Media

As it is impossible to reproduce exactly on the flat surface the appearance of any solid object, we have to think of the medium as a sensitive film on which certain aspects of reality may be transformed into line, colour or shading, which in their turn will be read as representation. This complex system of transmitting visual information presupposes knowledge – an ability to 'read' the message – on the part of the viewer as well as on that of the artist. We are making use of a sign-language, a sort of personal shorthand with which we may set down palpable phenomena so that in imagination we may walk round them, touch them, and, in the case of landscape, walk into them.

Paper

Only recently has work on paper come to be accepted as an autonomous art-form, not merely as an artist's sketch, a preparatory drawing or cartoon, subservient to the finished work, which is usually in a quite different medium.

The first to collect and keep drawings were the artists themselves, who found them most useful as a sort of optical data-bank, easy to store and to carry around. When going sketching, paper is also a most practical lightweight commodity, inexpensive, replaceable and easy to dispose of should the work be unsatisfactory.

In our time paper has become the most accessible piece of artists' material, due to mass-production, but the resulting standardization has made fine hand-made paper all the rarer.

Life-drawing is often a hit-and-miss affair, with many pages of the sketch-book being covered in a short time; there is often a lot of waste. This has meant that often fine work has been done on inferior material: most of Klimt's and Schiele's beautiful drawings were executed on cheap and yellowed packing-paper. There is nevertheless a sensual pleasure in handling and working with fine papers. They are also a better support for the varied markings made by the diverse implements of draughtsmanship, not to mention the very great difference when they are used for pigments such as watercolour, gouache or pastel.

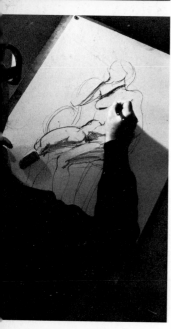

It is most useful to have a certain variety of papers to hand, especially in life-drawing where a uniformity of style and approach is to be avoided, and variations in media can often bring about new solutions.

It is beyond the scope of this book to give a run-down on all available papers; the information can be found elsewhere, the supply varies greatly from country to country, and choice is often limited, both for economic reasons and because many lines are being discontinued everywhere as traditional paper-making methods disappear. It is important to bear in mind, however, that there are still a great variety of whites to be listed under the name of 'white paper', ranging from an almost blinding snowy white to the just-off-grey of eggshell. Tinted papers range from the deepest black through practically the whole spectrum to the lightest yellow and off-white. Texture and grain vary from the brittle gloss of cardboard to the cloth-like quality of fine watercolour paper. Variety and experiment are essential.

Pencil

This simple and everyday implement can effect the most subtle gradations, from velvety black to the lightest of greys. Fine lines and intense patches of shading, spontaneous jottings, flamboyant lines and areas of painstaking detail can be

attained. It obeys every movement of the hand, responds to the lightest pressure. The lines may be softened and blurred by the fingers. There is practically no limit to the ways it can be moved over the paper: long flowing strokes as well as spontaneous jabs. It lies easily in the hand and transmits every idea instantaneously. It is easily erased, so work in pencil is always open to correction and revision. It is in many ways the ideal medium for drawing the nude. We can render lines, space, shadows directly; we can draw over the same areas again and again. Great variation in tone and intensity can be gained from the use of various thicknesses of lead.

Photographs of the author at work by Erich Lessing, Vienna 1974

Charcoal

This much more fugitive medium is relatively easy to apply, and with it we may cover larger areas. It will work well on the roughest and cheapest paper. Its advantages come out best when it is smudged by a finger, as when putting in zones of shadow or indicating form in a direct and rudimentary way. For quick sketching charcoal is most useful, but its drawbacks lie in a certain flatness and perhaps in its all too great facility in handling.

Crayon and chalk

A crayon combines the advantages of charcoal with the precision of a pencil: the blacks come out richer and it does not disappear if not sprayed with fixative. It can also be worked over with greater intensity than charcoal.

Sanguine, or red chalk, once standard life-class equipment, is nowadays much less used, although it does approximate to flesh tone. White chalk can be most effective in heightening drawings in pencil and crayon on tinted paper, picking out highlights or defining areas of concentrated light.

Pen and ink

To a much greater extent than in the previously mentioned techniques, the use of the pen determines the style of drawing. Since the pen can cover only a certain distance before it has to be dipped again, the lines or strokes are limited in length. There is thus a greater affinity to writing. The movement of the pen comes from the fingers and wrist and can be drawn in one direction only. The lines have a tendency to thicken towards the end of the stroke, and are thus well suited not only to delineating form but also to depicting movement. Shading can be formed by means of parallel lines, moving sometimes with, sometimes against the form, or by cross-hatching, or by clots and stipples. An equally effective method is to combine pen-drawn lines with washes of diluted Indian ink, whereby broad connecting areas of shadow are created.

Watercolour

This is perhaps the most difficult medium for the nude, as work in watercolours has to be executed with rapidity and decisiveness, correction being hardly possible.

It is a transparent medium, the white of the paper shining through. Water is used to dilute the pigment, and, what is more, to determine its intensity. To render the exact colouring of skin is laborious and at best insipidly naturalistic. An approximation of colours must be arrived at, a system of colour contrasts which will read as flesh-tints. Now, the best watercolour nudes are distinguished by a completely anti-naturalistic approach in colour: bluish highlights, olive greens, deep red shadows. This medium is a constant challenge to the colouristic inventiveness of the artist. As swift work is inevitable, the results, if successful (and this is not always the case even with the masters), possess a unique freshness and spontaneity.

Watercolour, and gouache as well, may sometimes be used to add colour-accents to a drawing executed in black and white. This sounds deceptively easy but carries with it the risk of ruining an otherwise good drawing. Colour as an addition should be used with the greatest discretion, and only where its introduction as a pictorial element lends a new dimension to the drawing.

Tempera and gouache

Unlike watercolour, these are opaque and can be painted over; they are useful in gaining more painterly effects, and the approximation to oil-painting is obvious. The pigment is flatter than watercolour and lacks its transparency and lustre.

Models

It is not easy to define a good model. The question seems deceptively easy to answer: a well-proportioned figure, good colouring, the ability to stand still and, of course, a healthy lack of inhibition with regard to taking one's clothes off. This theory has been disproved time and time again. A good model, male or female, may well have anything but a perfect figure. On the contrary, many artists have found physically most attractive persons an uninteresting subject to work from. Perhaps with working from the nude the same holds good as with portraiture: the departures from the norm, the unexpected, the unique, make depiction interesting. The body, like the face, is unique, bearing the markings of life and experience.

Beauty in art is the end-product, not necessarily the starting point. What then is beauty in a body? One of the most fascinating models I ever drew was a paunchy elderly man. On the other hand a very pretty girl with perfect shapes can stimulate any feeling but the one of wishing to draw or paint her. It is almost impossible to determine what constitutes good subject matter for art: the grand panoramic landscape or the corner of a back-yard, the smooth and appealing features of youth or the lined and worn face of age and experience. Study and interpretation of the human body means a certain freshness of approach, and concentration on just one particular type can lead to repetitiveness and mannerism. Every body is interesting – the quality of a model can be determined perhaps only in hindsight when confronted with the finished work.

The model must evoke something far more subtle than that which goes under the cliché of 'inspiration': the visual curiosity of the artist. For this a contribution on the model's part, if only a certain interest in the proceedings, can be a help. Absolute indifference has a tendency to transmit itself. 'Posing' is thus something indefinably more than just standing still.

The artist-model relationship is a system of delicate balances between commitment and aloofness, physical proximity and physical distance, excitement and sheer hard work. A strong relationship is almost inevitable, whether it extends to personal or sexual involvement or not. While some artists – Degas being the classic example – remain aloof, confining their involvement to the work in hand, seemingly ignoring their models, sexually attractive or not, to the point of rudeness, other artists practise life-drawing as a logical extension of their relationship with a particular person. Thus, Picasso's stylistic periods are invariably linked with the physical presence in his work of a succession of models, who were also to share his life. It is really a question of which stimulus is the more relevant to each widely differing creative temperament.

Posing

In life-drawing the pose is the position the model takes up for a limited period, which means that he or she has to hold reasonably still in order to be drawn. It has often been maintained that a 'natural' pose, rather than an 'academic' one, is a considerable help to the artist, and this is borne out by, for instance, the *figura serpentinata* of the Baroque. Both the 'academic' and the 'natural' have been the basis of many fine works, but I think the distinction no longer holds.

There is nothing 'natural' in standing or sitting unclothed in public, except perhaps in certain parts of Africa, Australia and the Amazon Valley. We all know the sensation of 'feeling naked', and this is considered an experience very much out of the ordinary. We have lost the innocence of the naked body, and the sight of a crowd of people on a nudist beach acting 'naturally' is often embarrassing. Of course, a marked change occurs when the body becomes the instrument of our emotions and our sensuality. Nakedness is experienced in the act of love, in clinical examination and, at another extreme, in the forced histrionic sexuality of the strip-show. All these factors, as well as the life-class itself, are valid material for observation and interpretation in art.

Let us now try to bring together a few basic rules:

1. The model should take up a pose that clearly brings out what the artist intends to draw. He may already have an idea of what he wishes to do before posing the model; or the pose may come about spontaneously.
2. The position should be chosen in such a manner that the model will not have to move or take a break for thirty to forty minutes, i.e. before the drawing is ready. Of course this does not arise with quick poses for the purpose of sketching.
3. When a break is needed, the model must be able to resume the identical pose. This is made easy by drawing a chalk line round the feet, leaving a mark into which the model can step after the break.
4. Lighting of the model is of utmost importance. Good lighting moulds the body and gives us more to draw; lack of it can make the best pose flat and insipid. If a movable source of light is available, it can be put to good use in lighting the model from various angles. There is a wealth of alternatives, from using daylight from several windows to posing the model against the light. With experience, good use can be made of shadows, subject of course to the technique employed: for a simple line-drawing, too much shadow is superfluous and even distracting, whereas in a wash-drawing, or any technique emphasizing form, shadow is vital.

Boeckl often worked with two or more models, and, in posing them, brought in a new sense of contrast: foreshortening, shadows, one model standing, the other reclining, proximity and distance. These group-poses are more difficult to draw; concentration on the essentials is always necessary and makes for training in selective vision. This contrasting of bodies stimulates new forms of composition and polarities of expression. Several figures in a composition inevitably introduce a narrative content, often completely unintended by the artist, purely on the strength of the many interpretative possibilities that suggest themselves to the viewer, who instinctively assumes that no two or more figures can be in proximity without some reason.

Oskar Kokoschka was displeased with the insipid and conventional work turned out by a group of students at the Salzburg Summer School. He told the model, a rather tired-looking man, to feign a collapse during a pose; which the model did most convincingly, to the great shock and consternation of the students. Kokoschka, after revealing the trick, told them always to remember that they were not drawing 'a model' but a human being of flesh and blood, and that he had planned this little shock-treatment to remind them of that essential fact.

In sketching from life, the pose, however statically held by the model in the course of change to a two-dimensional design, invariably indicates movement. This is also due to the way in which the viewer's gaze is directed along the drawing, moving from bigger to smaller, from sweeping lines and curves to smaller pictorial elements, light and shadow. Rodin's statement that movement is 'the transition from one pose to another' owes much to the introduction of photographic information on moving figures during the second half of the last century. Compared with these forerunners of cinematographic documentation, most depictions of movement in art (for example, Géricault's horses with all four legs clear of the ground simultaneously) were 'wrong'. And yet an arrested phase of motion just does not 'read' as movement, as a work of art does. It is the artist's synthetic combination of various elements in the motion of a given body which gives the impression that movement is being seen.

Starting

A sheet of paper, as yet unmarked, lies staring at us; the model has been posed, the stage is set. In this empty space the body will be placed, the surrounding space indicated. The composition of the figure on the paper must be reckoned before starting on the actual drawing. The figure has an obstinate tendency to grow beyond the edges of the paper, disappearing at either the neck or the legs. The other extreme is that the figure is so diminutive that it floats about on the sheet. Such failings will mar the best attempts and should be avoided at the outset. One way that I have found most useful is to begin the study by indicating two short pencil lines, one near the top of the paper, the other at the bottom. These determine the dimensions of the figure.

Now let us look at the model carefully. The pose is determined by various factors, and chiefly, if the model happens to be standing, by the distribution of body weight. Which leg is bearing the weight? The answer should be stressed from the very beginning.

The next possible step is to draw a series of connecting lines between the shoulders, the breasts, the hips, the knees and the feet. Now is the time to look closely for interrelating forms – breasts, belly, limbs – so as to determine how the light reveals their construction. It is wise to leave details until the next stage and to concentrate on finding a simple functional scheme to register proportions, an elementary roughing-in which may be altered at will.

As the drawing progresses, mistakes come to light, which should be corrected either by erasing or by working-over with stronger lines. The eraser is now as important an instrument as the pencil.

Suddenly, quite unexpectedly, details come to the fore, and, at a moment that is difficult to determine, the drawing itself takes over and develops its own momentum. The mind of the artist now takes on the function of controller, of critic. Parts of a drawing, though successful in themselves, prove to be damaging to the whole and have to be taken out. Slight corrections are now ineffective; a tentative re-setting of a line can be closer to the truth but immediately gives an undesired feeling of wariness. The best way to correct is to attack forcefully the offending portion of the drawing; to eliminate with a surgical ruthlessness, to overwork with surer and heavier lines and shading.

When drawing the seated figure it is important to consider the chair, or couch, or whatever the model is sitting on, as a basic element of the composition: it influences the way the weight of the body is distributed, and therefore the way the limbs are composed. Whatever we wish to express through our drawing, the act of sitting or reclining will be the first consideration. Without the chair or base to support the body, the drawing will not make sense.

As we are not confining ourselves to simply depicting the figure in a compositional vacuum, it will have to be given a position and a context. What most good drawings have in common is an indication of the space surrounding the figure, the floor on which it is standing or lying, the furniture on which it is seated. Sometimes this can be achieved simply by putting in shadow. Or the figure may of course be placed on the paper so well, overcoming the great difficulty of defining correctly the distance from the edges, that the surrounding space is self-evident.

It is most difficult to determine the exact point at which a drawing or painting has reached its optimal state, the moment when the artist ought to stop working. Each work arrives at a point beyond which it is imprudent to advance, as any addition can only be detrimental to the whole. But the artist will invariably have formed in advance a mental image of the subject; and experience in comparing this image with the state reached by a drawing in the course of execution is an essential element of creativity.

Six stages of the drawing shown in the photographs on pp. 8–9

Colour Plates

I Georges Rouault 1871–1958

Nude Doing up her Hair 1907
watercolour and pastel 30·8 x 30·5 cm (12⅛ x 12 in)
Musée d'Art Moderne de la Ville de Paris

She sits like a huge jug, a dominating presence, the
great curve of her back with the thickly defined
vertebrae widening towards the base. This ominous
figure is supported by a study chair, and beyond her is
a mass of heavy furniture. The modelling of the figure
is deeply felt, as if Rouault had built her up piece by
piece with sculptor's clay. Line is used emphatically
throughout, though it indicates direction more than
detail. The tapering-off of the figure towards the head is
stressed by the angles of her bent arms, and at the
base the heavy feet overlap. The woman's
monumentality, a huge, living organism in the cramped
space of the room, is not in the least an object of
desire, but rather of fascination, with underlying
feelings of both fear and compassion.

II Amedeo Modigliani 1884–1920

Caryatid c. 1913–15
pastel and crayon with wash 53 x 48·4 cm (20⅞ x 19 in)
Musée d'Art Moderne de la Ville de Paris

The elongated aspect of this crouching figure owes
much to African sculpture. One basic oval lozenge
form prevails in head, eyes, arms, thigh. The body is
framed in a broad band of colour, which intensifies the
strong decorative element of the composition.

III Jules Pascin 1885–1930

Venus from Behind 1924–25
gouache
Musée d'Art Moderne de la Ville de Paris

The beautifully rendered back dominates the
composition. This painting is much more than a study
– rather a piece of organized reality. There is also a
sense of melancholic intimacy, subtly expressed in the
delicate, yet morbid colouring of the flesh.
   The figure forms an integral part of an interior, which
has nothing of the studio about it: the furniture is also
characterized and corresponds to the massive forms of
the woman. The dry and flat application of the paint
with short and crisp brush strokes is sustained
throughout.

IV Egon Schiele 1890–1918

Nude with Mauve Stockings c. 1911
watercolour 45 x 31·4 cm (17¾ x 12⅜ in)
Collection Barbra Streisand

The artist may want to emphasize a particular detail,
lead the eye to that particular part of a drawing. In this
Schiele, for instance, the wildly gesturing legs – one
bare thigh fore-shortened, the other stretched out to
the jutting pelvis – and the sagging breasts, are all
grouped around the pubic hair as the focal point of
the design.
   Schiele's bizarre line and anguished ornamentation
are already there in this early drawing – as is the
strange balance between attraction and revulsion in
the somewhat feverish sexuality which pervades most
of his work.

V Oskar Kokoschka 1886–

Standing Nude c. 1921
watercolour 65 x 44 cm (25⅝ x 17⅜ in)
Albertina, Vienna

Broad horizontal strokes of warm ochre and sienna
model the body; a thick curved line accentuates the
left hip. This sturdy body is contrasted with its classical
contrapposto stance. The flesh is rendered exclusively
with warm earth-tones. The contrasting heavy and
light blues are confined to the background and help to
give form to the figure; they also define the space in
which it is situated.
   Kokoschka, one of the few great watercolour
painters of the century, has not made a drawing
heightened with colour, but has used the medium in a
wholly painterly way, letting the colours flow freely
from the brush, intermingling occasionally, but
inevitably defining the form. The red of the head-cloth
counter-balances the dark blue shadow around the
feet. Everything is part of a system of colour-washes,
beautifully contained on the sheet of paper.

VI George Segal 1924–

Untitled 1972
pastel 62·2 x 47 cm (24 ½ x 18 ½ in)
Courtesy Sidney Janis Gallery, New York

The broad expanse of a woman's back, viewed on a
monumental scale, with the vertebrae forming a deep
valley. This fragment more than fills the area of the
paper; the imagination extends the figure further in all
directions. The pastel medium is used to model the
forms from light to dark shadow in a painterly manner,
Segal using heavy lines only to indicate the shoulders
and hair.

VII Duncan Grant 1885–

Kneeling Nude
pastel over gouache on paper 29 x 18·7 cm (11 ⅜ x 7 ⅜ in)
Private collection

The paper plays an important part in this drawing. Its
brick-red gouache gives an indication of flesh tone; its
rough grain determines the character of the
draughtsmanship. The modelling of the body is
effected by the picking out of the highlights with white.
This, together with the bold, black strokes which define
the outline and enliven the background, imparts
plasticity and firmness.

VIII Francis Bacon 1909–

Lying Figure 1969
oil on canvas 198 x 147·5 cm (78 x 58 in)
Private collection, Montreal

Bacon preserves no drawings; but his oil paintings
reflect the quality of his observation of the nude. His
compositions often evolve from nudes of a particularly
intense, even painful vision. In spite of their distortion
they are immediately identifiable as human with all the
starkness of forensic specimens. They are invariably
placed in a spatial concept of an equally alienating
aspect, a void rather than a room.

Bacon's images of naked bodies owe much to
Muybridge's sequential photographs of human bodies
in motion, which anticipated the veracity of the film-
camera nearly a hundred years ago. As John Russell
has pointed out, these are for Bacon a 'point of
departure'. The sense of movement is often arrested as
in a photograph, and we are left with the feeling of
before and after deliberately blocked out.

The impasto of the flesh-tones has a vitality all its
own and is contrasted with broad zones of flat,
impersonal pigment.

VII

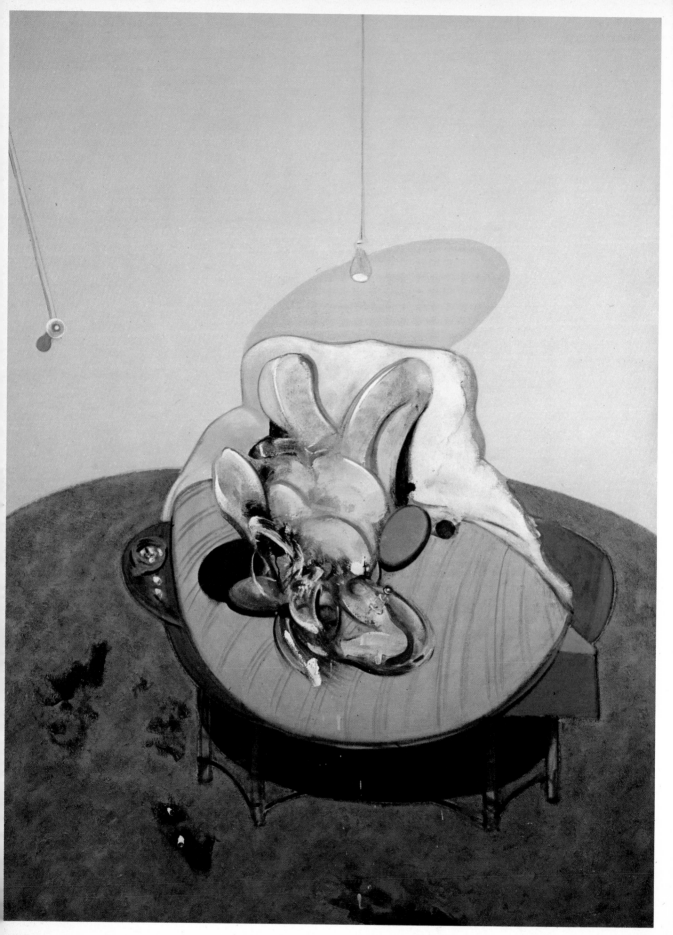

Georges Rouault 1871–1958

Study for 'The Ordeal of Samson' 1893
pencil 20 x 8 cm (7 ⅞ x 3 ⅛ in)
Private collection, Paris

This very early drawing of a dramatically posed
man reveals Rouault's origin in nineteenth-century
Romanticism. An expressive, strong line forms the
torso, the legs are more sketchily treated. It is the
left arm, bent at the elbow, the hand resting on
the hip, the strong suggestion of muscle and
movement, which impart to this figure its arresting
vitality. This is draughtsmanship in the classical
manner which, once mastered, Rouault was soon
to abandon, having developed his own
characteristic style.

Paul Klee 1879–1940

Nude in School of Painting 1906
pencil 11 x 13 cm (4⅜ x 5⅛ in)
Paul Klee Stiftung, Kunstmuseum, Bern

A wry humour characterizes this drawing. Thin spidery lines
define the model, who is posed, bearing a long-stemmed
flower, in an exaggerated classical stance. Around her are
grouped the art-students in perpetual, somewhat desperate
motion – wraith-like figures surrounding the nude.

This strange mixture of poetic line and satire is typical of
much of Paul Klee's work of this period. On the borderline
of abstraction, at this stage the human body is still clearly
discernible in his drawings.

Albert Marquet 1875–1947

Nude c. 1910–12. Brush and black ink 30·6 x 22·2 cm (12 x 8¾ in)
National Gallery of Canada, Ottawa

Marquet's nudes have a brittle elegance all their own. They are linear drawings,
but mostly executed with the brush, and do not rely on the precision of pen-
work. Drawing with the brush is a most direct method – little being left for after-
thoughts. The jet-black line of the brush-end freshly dipped into the indian ink
contrasts strongly with the dry broken line achieved when most of the ink has
left the brush.

Marquet manages to draw in a painterly manner with an utmost economy of
means, outlining the figure, giving minimal indications of furniture, of the space
in which the model is placed. We can follow the direction of each brush stroke,
our eyes moving with the painter's hand.

Pierre Bonnard 1867–1947

Woman in a Tub 1922. Pencil 23 x 18·1 cm (9 x 7 ⅛ in)
Musée du Louvre, Paris, gift of George Besson

The nude is seen as an integral part of a composition. The body is fixed in its place by a complex network of vertical and horizontal elements, not only indicating various pieces of furniture but also giving spatial depth. The figure is executed in a system of short pencil lines, the form drawn and re-drawn, leaving no suggestive single lines but giving more a blurred outline, stressing the form. Shadows emerge from a seemingly wilful criss-crossing of pencil strokes. Although this is a linear drawing, Bonnard achieves by the use of a simple soft lead-pencil an amazing range of values of tone. Building up his composition from small elements of short pencil strokes, Bonnard bathes the figure in a vibrating indirect light.

Georges Minne 1866–1941

Nude Mother and Child 1918
crayon 36 x 25 cm (14 ⅛ x 9 ⅞ in)
Musées Royaux des Beaux-Arts de Belgique,
Brussels

The soft roundness of the limbs and the
arched back are contrasted with the marked
angularity of the pose. The Belgian sculptor
uses the crayon to maximum effect: the
forms are worked up from delicate shadings,
the grain of the paper giving the darker areas
a vibrating, tactile quality.

Augustus John 1878–1961

Nude Study c. 1906. Pencil 48·3 x 29·2 cm (19 x 11 ½ in). Collection Peter Harris

Once idolized, then considered too academic, John's drawings are now admired
again for their elegance and craftsmanship.

This drawing is in many ways a typical work by the artist: a strong feeling for
harmony of movement, exact observation of detail and proportion. The pencil is
employed with the greatest delicacy: long sweeping lines, softly rounded forms,
detailing (the vertebrae and muscles of the back, the beautifully rendered foot of
the weight-bearing leg) and an overall harmony. Nothing is out of place and no
jarring note occurs. Great attention is given to hands and feet – usually the most
difficult parts to draw. The beauty of the woman is perhaps somewhat
overstressed for to-day's taste, but this is more than compensated for by the
artist's superb command of the means employed.

Auguste Rodin   1840–1917

Seated Nude, after 1900. Pencil 34·3 x 27·6 cm (13 ½ x 10 ⅞ in)
Courtauld Institute Galleries, London

'I can work only from the model,' said Rodin. His method of life-drawing was fundamentally anti-academic. He practised a veritable cult of the nude model. His studio was populated by numerous men, women and children in constant natural motion – a sort of indoor nudist colony; the sculptor moving among them, executing rapid sketches. Rodin abhorred static poses, inducing his models to move freely, conditioning himself to the constant presence of naked people.

Rodin's life-drawings are invariably distinguished by a great spontaneity and sense of movement. An expressive, flowing outline encloses the body; shading is sparingly, if ever, used. Rodin frequently filled in the outlines with washes of watercolour.

Auguste Rodin 1840–1917

Reclining Nude c. 1900. Pencil 31 x 20 cm (12 ¼ x 7 ⅞ in). Musée Rodin, Paris

Fernand Léger 1881–1955

Study of Male Nude 1909. Pencil 33 x 25 cm (13 x 9 ⅞ in)
Musée National d'Art Moderne, Paris, gift of D.-H. Kahnweiler

Léger's early linear drawing of a male nude already displays a certain gravity
which was subsequently to characterize much of his work.

   The seated woman, an essay in Cubism, with which Léger was linked for a
short period, is typical of the Cubist approach to the depiction of the human
figure. Not only is the body reduced to stereometric elementary forms such as
cube, ball and cone; there is also the new element of being able to apprehend
each form three-dimensionally as it links up with its neighbouring components
into an interlocking anthropomorphic image.

   With Léger's drawing, as with all major Cubist work, we have the uncanny
feeling of taking up several viewpoints simultaneously, of being able literally to
see around corners. And yet there is no jigsaw-puzzle effect. Léger's functional
simplicity reflects his later fascination with the artifacts developed from the new
materials of industrial society.

Fernand Léger 1881–1955

Nude Woman, Seated 1912. Pencil 64 x 49 cm (25 ¼ x 19 ¼ in). Private collection, Canada

1922-23

Alberto Giacometti 1901–66

Seated Nude from Behind 1922–23
pencil 48·5 x 31·5 cm (19 ⅛ x 12 ⅜ in)
Alberto Giacometti-Stiftung, Kunsthaus,
Zürich

In this early drawing Giacometti views
the body as a system of clearly defined
planes. The dividing line between light
and shadow is drawn with great
emphasis, shaping the figure into inter-
relating segments.

Alberto Giacometti 1901–66

Standing Nude 1955. Pencil 64 x 48 cm (25 ¼ x 18 ⅞ in)
The Robert and Lisa Sainsbury Collection

'I would like to render woman as a sort of Marilyn Monroe; but she always turns
out narrower and longer with me.' Giacometti speaks of MM here as the
universally recognizable female idol of the 1950s, and this is no mere catch-
phrase: the making of the feminine idol of our time was very much the artist's
concern.

In all its starkness this figure is a most sensitive and complicated mechanism:
the naked human is seen as a symbol of existence achieved through observation
of painful acuteness. This great sensitivity flows through the whole figure, starting
with the head and face with its expression of wide-eyed urgency, continuing
downward – the form being stated by bundles of crisp vertical lines, moving
closely together for the shadows, bunching at the joints, terminating in
elongated feet reminiscent of a Crucifixion.

Gustav Klimt 1862–1918

Standing Nude c. 1914. Pencil 58·6 x 37·3 cm (23 ⅛ x 14 ⅝ in)
Graphische Sammlung der Albertina, Vienna

A gently undulating line caresses the body more than it describes it. It is
characteristic of Klimt's later style that background and environment disappear
and an evocative, almost lyrical mood takes their place. And yet there is nothing
schematic about this drawing, clearly that of a particular woman, whom the
artist succeeds in portraying with the greatest economy of means.

Gustav Klimt 1862–1918

Seated Nude. Pencil 56 x 37 cm (22 x 14½ in)
Galerie Welz, Salzburg

This openly erotic drawing achieves an almost sculptural presence without the
use of shading. The woman is provocatively posed: chin on hand, the elbow
resting on the knee, the other arm in a bold angle, the legs wide apart. The
expressive face is surmounted by a mass of hair, and a summary attempt at
ornamentation is made in the couch on which the model is seated.

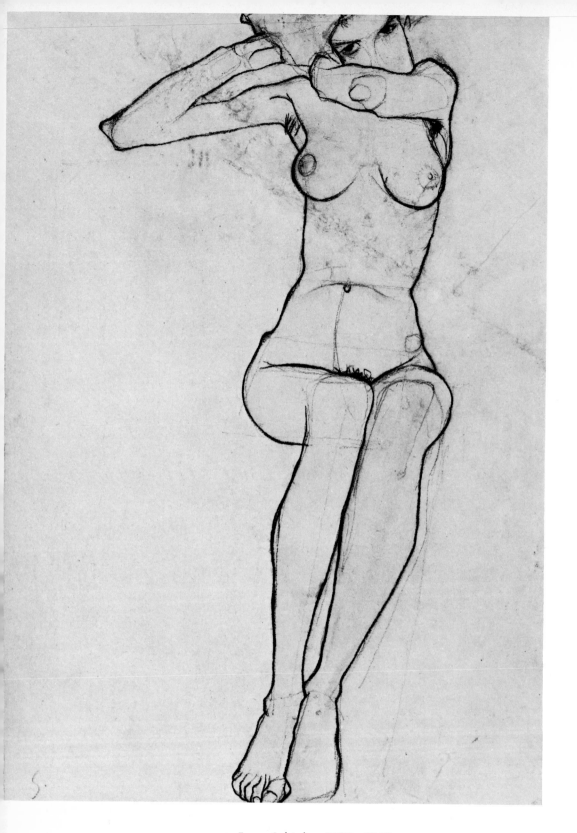

Egon Schiele   1890–1918

Seated Nude 1910. Pencil 44·5 x 31·5 cm (17 ½ x 12 ⅜ in)
Galerie Michael Pabst, Vienna

The figure is placed right of centre, and with the exception of the raised arms
describes a closed and angular form throughout. The outline is more rigidly in
agreement with factual appearance than is the case in the artist's later work.
There are only occasional definitions of plasticity, such as the curved vertical line
leading downwards from the navel.

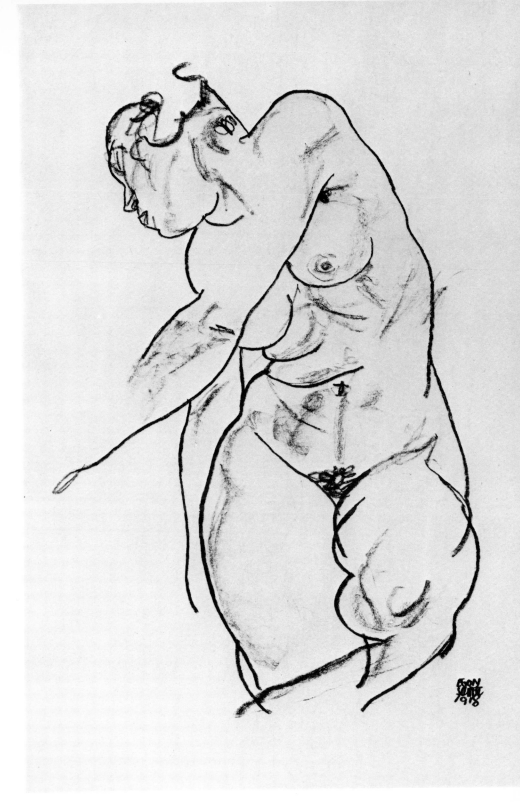

Egon Schiele   1890–1918

Nude leaning to the Right 1918. Crayon, 47 x 31·5 cm (18 ½ x 12 ⅜ in)
Galerie Michael Pabst, Vienna

The flowing lines achieve an ornamental quality typical of the artist's late style.
His models seem now to have put on more flesh, are more sensuously rounded
and provoking rather than provocative. The soft crayon is now the congenial
instrument, rather than the harder, more obstinate pencil and pen of his earlier
work.

Henri Matisse   1869–1954

Reclining Nude 1936
indian ink

Woman is here seen as ornament, the body lying on the floral pattern, its long
flowing lines set off by the smaller, equally linear elements of leaves and flowers.
   For Matisse supreme drawing was not an accessory of painting, but rather an
autonomous art-form. These purely linear, almost calligraphic drawings need no
colour or shading. It is amazing that, without any variation of thickness, the pure
line can evoke such plasticity and three-dimensional form. The drawings have
been brought to an overall degree of completion throughout: not one line, it
seems, could be added or taken away.

Henri Matisse 1869–1954

Kneeling Nude 1936. Indian ink 56·5 x 38·5 cm (22 ¼ x 15 ⅛ in)
Musée d'Art Moderne de la Ville de Paris

Pablo Picasso 1881–1973

Bathers 1918. Pencil 24·1 x 31·1 cm (9 ½ x 12 ¼ in)
Courtesy of the Fogg Art Museum, Harvard University
Bequest of Meta and Paul J. Sachs

These large-limbed women are from Picasso's neoclassical
period, so-called because they are in some way reminiscent of
classical or rather Hellenistic sculpture and vase-paintings – but
also of Poussin's figure-groups.

   There is much weight and gravity in these bodies, the
draughtsmanship wholly confined to outlines of equal thickness.
There is a great finality and decisiveness in this work, nothing of
the spontaneous sketch, the building up of a composition from
small elements; nor is there any indication of shadow. The
staggering effect of three-dimensionality owes much to Picasso's
Cubist period. But the most important element is the artist's
supreme competence: nothing in this drawing is the product
of re-consideration, of second thoughts; it is an aggressive
statement of mastery. The individual figures form a frieze-like
circular composition, in which a line becomes the horizon and
empty space becomes the sky. Everything is irrevocable: the
viewer does not for one moment feel that this is a slice of life,
that the women will ever shift position.

Jules Pascin 1885–1930

Two Nudes 1926. Pencil 48·9 x 41·9 cm (19 ¼ x 16 ½ in)
Philadelphia Museum of Art. Given by Richard Davis

A domestic little brothel-scene – two girls taking a break, the naked one reclining on an upholstered chair whose outlines echo her own well-padded contours. They are drawn with tender interest: long flowing lines defining the form, lines that vary in thickness, supported by little patches of shading. There is also a very sensual, tactile quality in this drawing: the flesh is set off against the folds of the chemise in the figure on the left (what a splendid thick haunch!); on the naked one the mask-like face is set in crisp wavy hair. This tender interest of the artist also establishes a certain tense relationship between the two figures; their lassitude is not without a powerful erotic awareness of the viewer and of each other.

Otto Dix   1891–1969

Reclining Woman 1923. Indian ink 48 x 39·5 cm (18 ⅞ x 15 ½ in)
Collection Alfred Hrdlicka, Vienna

Art is not the falsification of experience but its expansion.
Konrad Fiedler

This is in many ways a strange drawing. Beauty of line and formal mastery are
employed to create an object of revulsion; there is little compassion here, rather
horrified sympathy with a fly-blown, abject specimen of humanity. And yet
the sheer nobility of the draughtsmanship gives us an almost Brechtian sense of
alienation, which transforms this piece of social surgery into a work of art.

Dix's brutal honesty and old-master command of technique are exemplified in
his drawings of the 1920s, when he was at the height of his powers. His style of
intense naturalism and concern with the everyday life of the down-and-out in
Weimar Germany is centred in his study of the underworld of small-time pimps
and worn-out prostitutes. In his tremendous war-paintings, he had portrayed the
wrecked and decaying bodies of soldiers in the trenches; his women are also
seen as victims, their bodies bearing every mark of destruction and decay. And
yet there is an open fascination about these drawings, an ambivalence that rules
out the possibility of sentimental moralizing.

Otto Dix 1891–1969

Standing Nude. Pencil 72 x 49 cm (28 ⅜ x 19 ¼ in). Collection Alfred Hrdlicka, Vienna

Handling the pencil with the precision of a surgeon's scalpel, Dix imparts to this
woman, with her obvious lack of conventional beauty, a certain morbid grace.
The heavy hips, the large pendulous breasts, are recorded with a cool
fascination; there is nothing grotesque about this figure.

George Grosz 1893–1959

Female Nude 1914
indian ink 32 x 24 cm (12 ⅝ x 9 ½ in)
Galerie Michael Pabst, Vienna

This torso is very much the drawing of a
particular person: face, breasts and fleshy
thighs are highly individualized. The
technique limits the pen and brush
strokes to a sparse recording of fact,
balancing brutality and tenderness.

Max Beckmann 1884–1950

Reclining Nude 1929. Charcoal 62·5 x 47·5 cm (24 ⅝ x 18 ¾ in). Collection Sprengel,
Hanover

Beckmann frames the body with a severe outline, and the shading is equally
direct. Strong emphasis is placed on the setting, of which the naked woman is
the dominant but by no means the sole constituent. The body intersects the
lines of blanket, cushion and bed, and the feet and left elbow are cut off by the
edge of the paper. Such confinement of the body within a restricted space adds
to its erotic presence. In spite of its rigid stylization, this is not a schematic,
anonymous construction but rather the depiction of a particular woman in a
personal context.

Oskar Kokoschka 1886–

Female Nude 1953. Crayon and pencil 58·5 x 44·5 cm (23 x 17 ½ in)
Collection Mrs Leonard S. Meranus, Cincinnati, Ohio

Kokoschka's characteristic expressive, broken line gives this seated figure
plasticity and gravity. The knees and thighs are emphasized with pencil strokes,
contrasting with the continuous outline running downwards from the neck to
the thigh.

Henri Gaudier-Brzeska 1891–1915

Seated Nude. Ink
Formerly Valeza Gallery

Gaudier-Brzeska's stylo-pen drawings show strong calligraphic character: the nude is written into the paper as with a ball-point pen. It also disproves the contention that sculptors' drawings are easily identifiable by their accentuation of form. Gaudier's nudes are the direct opposite: rapid jottings, spontaneous observations, the body composed in a closed, formal pattern of elegant and evocative thin lines.

Paul Delvaux 1897–

Adoration. Indian ink 23·5 x 32·5 cm (9 ¼ x 12 ¾ in)
Collection Dr and Mrs Stanley Finger, St Louis, Mo.

The Belgian Surrealist contrasts four nude figures with an alienated setting: a
stone wall blocks off the right half of the composition, on the left are indications
of a hilly landscape in the far background.

As a counterpoint to the nakedness of the women there is a man dressed in
hat and overcoat on the left.

There are two patches of intense darkness achieved through cross-hatching
pen strokes: the area separating the upper part of the two nudes in the right
foreground and the head and shoulders of the man. The figures are contained
within simple lines, with brief indications of shading.

André Masson 1896–

The Cascade 1938. Ink 46 x 35·2 cm (18 ⅛ x 13 ⅞ in)

This metamorphosis of landscape into woman, with its erotic evocation, is
characteristic of Masson's associative way of drawing. The anthropomorphic
forms perceived in various objects (not an uncommon practice) are here
deliberately sublimated. The simple and elegant line is used to convey the
subject matter with great directness. If there were more distortion of basic
human proportion, the viewer might easily miss the point. Surrealist drawing
is frequently as straightforward as possible, as its main object is to *describe*
phenomena rather than to interpret them.

This transition of earth, rock and vegetation into a female form seems to
possess something of the quality of a descriptive diagram.

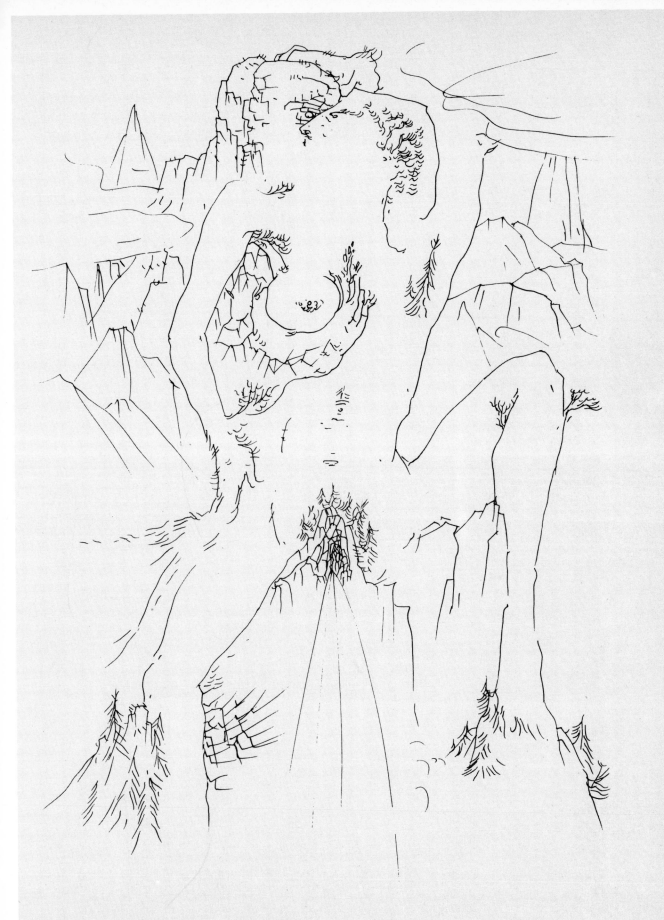

F Wotruba

Fritz Wotruba 1907–75

Two Studies of Reclining Nude 1950. Pencil 22 x 34 cm (8⅝ x 13⅜ in)
Late collection of the artist

These two studies of a reclining nude are more directly concerned with nature
than that reproduced on the next page-opening; the pencil clearly defines the
shape and density of the woman's body.

Jackson Pollock 1912–56

Untitled c. 1931–34. Crayon 46 x 30·5 cm (18⅛ x 12 in)
Collection Lee Krasner Pollock, New York

At first glance Pollock's nudes of the early 1930s are straightforward life-studies.
Yet a certain explosive quality is already discernible in this early work, clearly
under the influence of the Mexican muralist José Clemente Orozco. The bodies
are eminently three-dimensional, the individual forms heavily accentuated. A
muscular energy pervades; the draughtsmanship is firm and decisive.

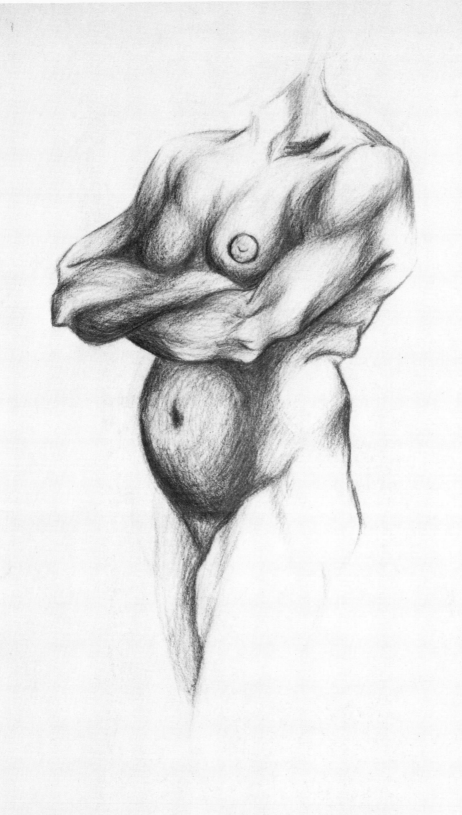

Ben Shahn

Ben Shahn *1898–1969*

Nude Girl, Back View 1928. Ink 40 x 29·8 cm (15¾ x 11¾ in)
Joseph Devernay Contemporary Art, New York

The massive, chunky figure of the girl kneeling on a bed is drawn with great
directness. The shading, with heavy short pen strokes, follows the form which is
also emphasized by the repeated re-tracing of the outline. There is much
movement in this figure, the distribution of the weight thrusting down from the
torso to be contained by the left knee and the right foot – a direct statement of
volume and movement with no regard for elegance of execution.

Fritz Wotruba *1907–75*

Study for Sculpture 1973. Pencil 21·5 x 36 cm (8½ x 14⅛ in)
Late collection of the artist

This drawing demonstrates the transition from nature to sculpture. The figure on
the right is a closely observed study of a man's legs and feet, one placed before
the other as in the act of walking. The other two figures transform this direct
statement of overlapping outlines, indicating muscles and sinews, into another
material and formal statement. The upper part of the figure grows out of the
hips, almost in the form of a tree-trunk; the movement of the life-drawing is
changed to sculptural stability.

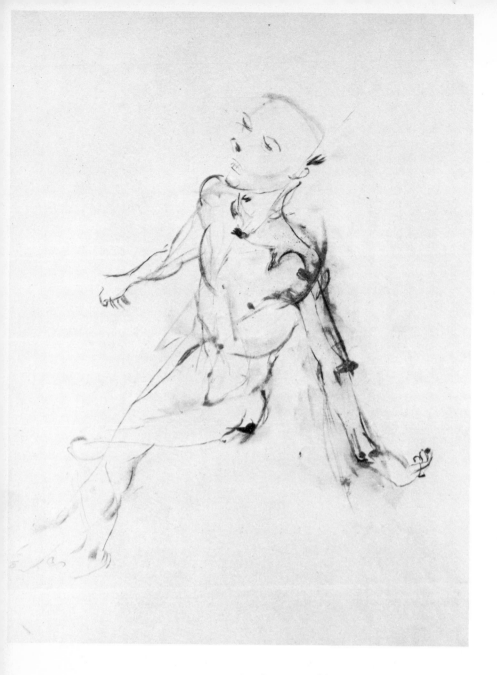

Herbert Boeckl 1894–1966

Nude Man Resting on his Arms 1919. Charcoal 48 x 36 cm (18 ⅞ x 14 ⅛ in)
Collection Maria Boeckl, Vienna

The male figure seems to lean out of the drawing towards the viewer. Boeckl
establishes points of anatomical reference – collar-bone, wrist and elbow – and
with great economy of means builds up the drawing, his charcoal stick moving
with the form. Those accentuated parts of the figure underline the functional
aspects of the pose, the trapeze-form of the arms bearing the weight of the
trunk, the muscles of the neck supporting the raised head.

All Boeckl's life-drawings are distinguished by a strong physical presence. He is
truly concerned with interpreting life in terms of human bodies, of the beauty of
functioning muscle and bone, and with the tactile aspects of flesh, as well as the
knowledge of what lies behind it. His nudes speak a physical language; the
technical means chosen are those that can best achieve lucidity.

Boeckl is not concerned with beauty of line, as his predecessors Klimt and
Schiele were; he always sees the body in the context of space and draws 'from
within': he builds up his figures from a structural core. The surface thus takes on
a strongly moulded, modelled aspect.

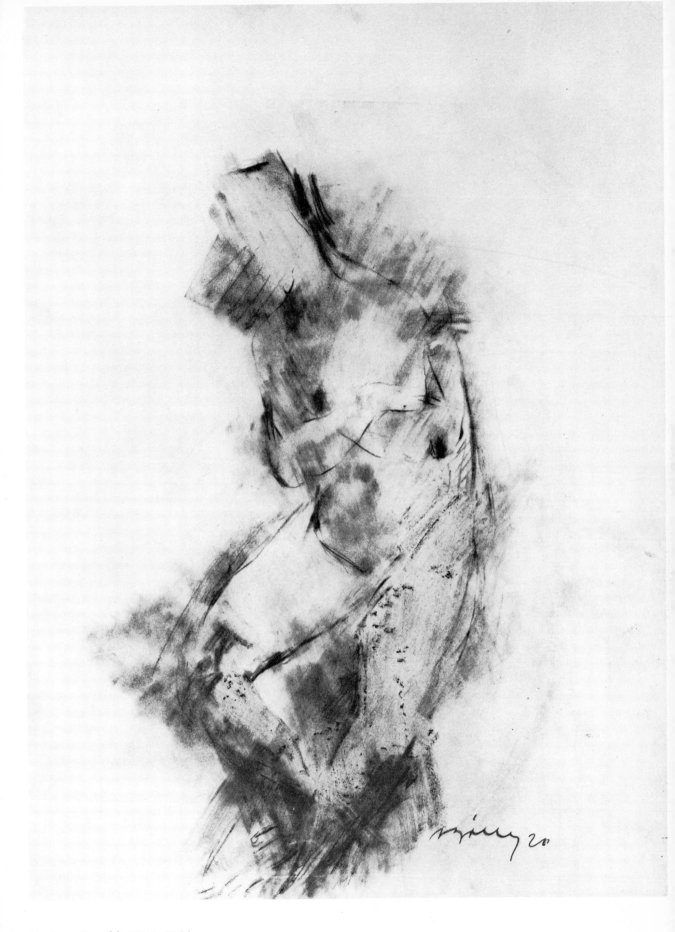

Herbert Boeckl 1894–1966
Female Nude 1920. Charcoal 48·9 x 36·7 cm (19 ¼ x 14 ½ in). Bibliothèque Nationale, Paris

Alfred Hrdlicka   1928–

Running Man 1970. Ink 48 x 63 cm (18⅞ x 24¾ in)
Collection of the artist

This emphatically unattractive man, caught in abrupt and jerking motion has an aggressive vitality, a plebeian arrogance, which is characteristic for much of Hrdlicka's work. The functionality of bone and muscle is stressed: there is an urgency about this figure, defined by flowing yet jagged outline and by the short hacking pen strokes of the shading.

   Hrdlicka, with Schönwald, Martinz and myself, was a pupil of Herbert Boeckl at the Vienna Academy in the years after the Second World War.

Alfred Hrdlicka   1928–

A Group 1973. Ink 67 x 48·5 cm (26⅜ x 19⅛ in)
Collection of the artist

These closely grouped figures constitute a forceful pattern of inter-relating forms.
The draughtsmanship is straightforward: outlines, with parallel strokes for the shadows. Proximity does not read as intimacy; the entangled naked bodies convey a sense of insecurity.

Rudolf Schönwald

Seated Nude 1949. Pencil 52 x 38 cm (20 ½ x 15 in)
Collection F. A. Morat, Freiburg im Breisgau

The borderline between light and shadow constitutes the form, the shading
never moving beyond this limitation. The light thus appears in greater intensity,
and models the forms of breasts, belly and thighs; the darker areas add volume
and density. The figure thus acquires its pronounced three-dimensionality and
physical presence.

Georg Eisler 1928–

Three Women 1968. Pencil 85 x 65 cm (33 ½ x 25 ⅝ in). Collection of the artist

Georg Eisler 1928–

Two Nude Studies 1969
pencil 50 x 65 cm (19⅝ x 25⅝ in)
Private Collection, Vienna

Georg Eisler 1928–

Seated Nude 1959
pencil 21 x 14 cm (8¼ x 5½ in)
Private Collection, Vienna

Balthus   1908–
(Balthazar Klossowski de Rola)

Study for 'Nude with Cat' *c*. 1954
ink and pencil 30·2 x 45·1 cm (11 ⅞ x 17 ¾ in)
Collection The Museum of Modern Art,
New York. Gift of John S. Newberry

This study for the painting now in
Melbourne does not place the figure in the
centre, but integrates it into an interior.
Balthus's nude is not the study of a body,
but rather the definition of a situation in
which the nakedness of the girl has strong
associative significance.

 The drawing of the figure with its strong
cross-hatched shading is more a statement
of fact than a study – it is to be viewed only
in the context of the room in which it takes
up the dominating position.

 In this evocation of a mood, 'setting up an
immediate emotional vibration' (John
Russell), Balthus demonstrates an original
creative approach. The outstretched girl,
arm thrusting upwards, finds a contrast in
the cat that appears over the back of the
chair, extending its paw downwards – a
charming device with somewhat sinister
undertones.

 The two slight sketches at the side show
alternative possibilities of poses.

Fritz Martinz 1924–

Standing Man, Back View. Crayon 67·5 x 45 cm (26 ⅝ x 17 ¾ in)
Collection of the artist

This forceful drawing is a detailed study of the relief-map of a man's back and also reveals the function of muscle and sinew. The action of pulling on the shirt sets in motion the system of distribution of balance, carried through from the shoulders to the heel of the weight-bearing right leg.

Francisco López 1932–

Male Nude 1973. Pencil 108 x 78 cm (42 ½ x 30 ¾ in)
Galerie Meyer-Ellinger, Frankfurt am Main

This obsessively detailed drawing utilizes the most elementary medium, pencil
on paper, to the utmost. With the exception of the head, every visible part of
the body is portrayed with the veracity of a camera-lens. This all-encompassing
building-up of the body, item by item, bristling with detail, also serves as an
essential element of alienation. This study from life can thus be read as a
comment on physical awareness.

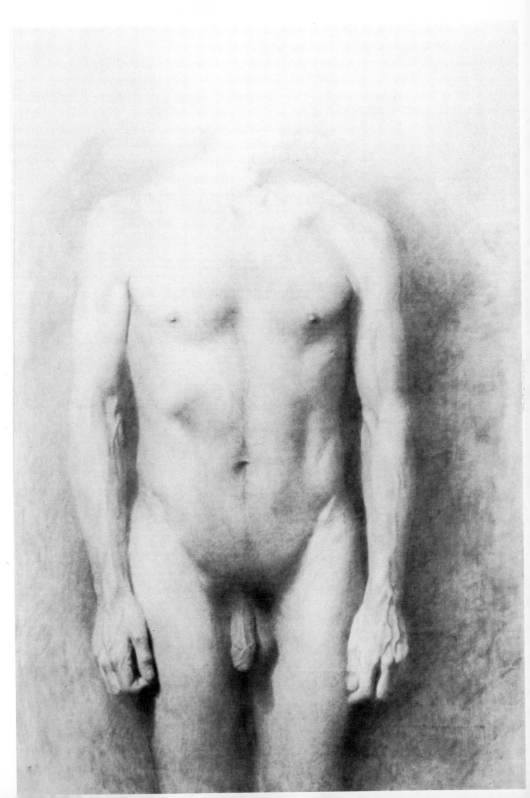

Henry Moore 1898–

Seated Nude, Life Drawing 1927. Ink and crayon 41·9 x 33·8 cm (16 ½ x 13 ⅜ in)
Collection Mr and Mrs Gordon Bunshaft

This drawing is the portrait of an arm, massive, bearing the weight of the seated
body, surmounted by a face of contrasting sensitivity. The rest of the body, with
the exception of the visible left breast, is rendered in line. It is the arm which
immediately demands attention, the shading beginning with delicate cross-
hatching and growing even darker, indicating the light working its way round
from the other side of the form. The fingers go out like roots into the ground;
this effect is stressed by the heavy dark lines appearing from under the figure –
an indication of shadow and at the same time of the cloth on which the woman
is seated.

   It would be easy to describe this as a typical 'sculptor's drawing'; but, like
most of Moore's nudes, it goes beyond that, existing in its own right as the work
of a supreme draughtsman. Exact observation, and the ability to see 'in the
round', are the pre-requisites of the sculptor thinking three-dimensionally; but
the composition of this figure in space, the accentuation of its elements, the
dramatic contrast of shadow and line, make it far more than a sculptor's study.

Henry Moore 1898–

Drawing from Life, Seated Figure 1933. Ink, wash and pencil 55·9 x 38·1 cm (22 x 15 in)
Collection Dr Alan Wilkinson, Toronto

The relatively small head and shoulders, contrasted with the monumental and
intensely shaded legs and feet, give this figure a strong feeling of depth. The
sculptural character owes much to the clearly defined distance from the knees
to the head.

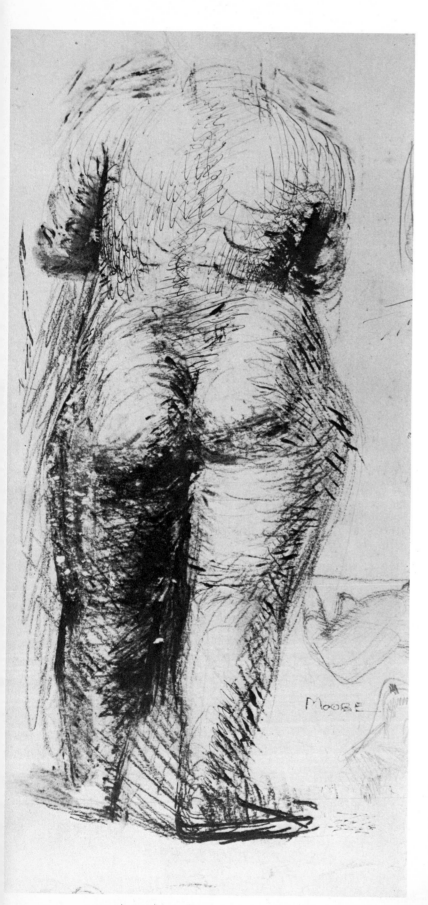

Henry Moore 1898–

Standing Figure 1926
ink and chalk 43·2 x 20·3 cm (17 x 8 in)
Collection Miss Mary Moore

A dense system of shading is applied here with the intensity and three-dimensional directness of sculptor's clay. The massive forms project themselves outward from the flat background towards the spectator.

Constant Permeke 1886–1952

The Two Sisters c. 1925
charcoal 180 x 116 cm (70 ⅞ x 45 ⅝ in)
Collection Louis Bogaerts, Brussels

The heavy-limbed women in this monumental drawing exemplify a physical presence which goes beyond a nature study. For all its close concurrence with the distribution of light and shadow on a woman's back, this drawing is also an expression of mood incurred by the posture and placing of two contrasting figures.

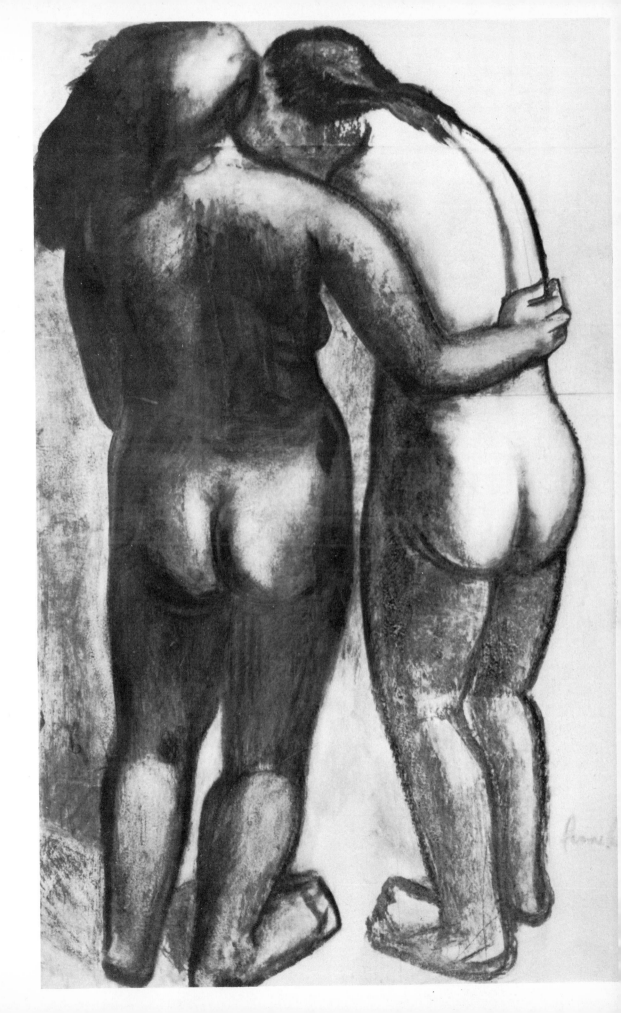

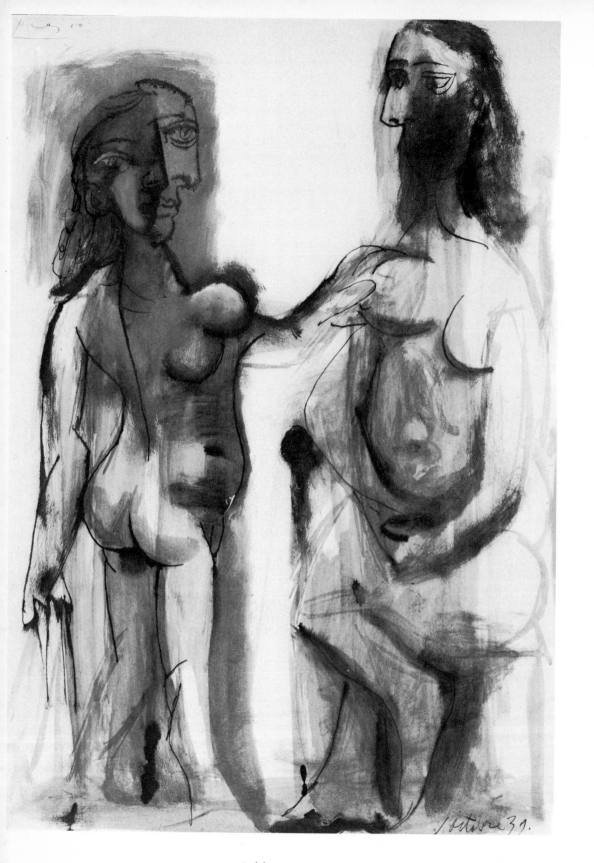

Pablo Picasso 1881–1973

Standing and Seated Nudes 1939. 62·5 x 46 cm (24 5/8 x 18 1/8 in). Galerie Beyeler, Basle

This confrontation of two monumental figures demonstrates Picasso's ability to display the human body simultaneously from various viewpoints. These figures never lose their organic cohesion and logic: on the contrary, the distortions give a unique element of three-dimensionality.

Willem de Kooning 1904–

Woman 1953. Crayon 91·4 x 61·4 cm (36 x 24 ⅛ in). Collection of Ms Ethel Scull

De Kooning's fierce and furious woman exemplifies what the English historian of art John Willett terms 'the figurative side of Abstract Expressionism'. The distortion is explosively violent, and yet the basic human proportions are not negated and there is a strong plastic, tactile quality, an almost Cubist feeling of being able to see around each form. These women of de Kooning's are twentieth-century fetishes of sexual aggression, on the borderline of abstraction and figuration, attraction and repulsion.

Giacomo Manzù 1908–

Bust 1956. Charcoal 35 x 55 cm (13¾ x 21⅝ in)
Formerly Hanover Gallery, London

The reclining figure is indicated by the right arm up to the elbow, and by the breast over which the head emerges. The modelling is slight and all the more effective – there is little more than an indication of nakedness. Manzù concentrates our interest on the oval of the face. It is an intimate study, almost a portrait. There is strong feeling of physical attraction enhanced by a great economy of means. If we abstract the head, the few lines forming the body could also give shape to a landscape.

Renato Guttuso 1912–

Standing Nude with Raised Arms c. 1960. Mixed Media 101 x 71 cm (39¾ x 28 in)
Collection Dr Peter Müller, Vienna

This large drawing combines robustness with elegance. The impulsive lines travel down the girl's back; the hips flare out to a splendid pear-shape, intensified by bold splotches of shadow. Face and breast appear in profile; there is even a bold stab at portraiture. The heavy shading of the hair is continued down alongside the torso, giving it by contrast a strong light. The half-tone washes give further indication of form.

Ennio Morlotti 1910–

Study for Nudes 1960. Pencil 35 x 49 cm (13¾ x 19¼ in)
Collection Dr Enrico Brambilla Pisoni

This drawing demonstrates the evolution of a life sketch
in various stages of realization. Morlotti begins at the
right by measuring out the proportions of the figure with
vertical and horizontal lines. Form is stated with diagonal
pencil strokes which pick out the figure from the
background. The two figures in the middle show a
more detailed approach: the background shading is
connected with the shadows of the body, which are
stated in a spontaneous and free-flowing system of
pencil strokes, the roughness of the paper giving a soft
and broken texture.

Josef Erhardy 1928–

Bending Forward 1972. Wash 33·5 x 21 cm (13 ⅛ x 8 ¼ in). Galerie Ariel, Paris

The American sculptor relates surface to form, the inner edge of the arms and the outer edge of the thigh forming strong vertical elements which support the trunk with its soft folds of flesh and pendulous breasts.

Shading is used to underline the form; all the brushwork is kept within the contours of the body.

Leonard Baskin 1922–

Watching Man 1975. Ink and wash 78·7 x 59·7 cm (31 x 23 ½ in)
Courtesy of Kennedy Galleries, Inc., New York

The watcher is neither young nor attractive. Baskin contrasts the expression of tense expectancy on the man's face with the pointedly unathletic, flabby body. Short, parallel pen strokes give an indication of form, and the outline is drawn with a certain reluctant negation of elegance – the physical characteristics being matched by the non-fluency of the linear composition, which conveys a feeling of urgency. The face and the hand are drawn with melancholic detail. The body has a certain instability; a sense of danger is apparent.

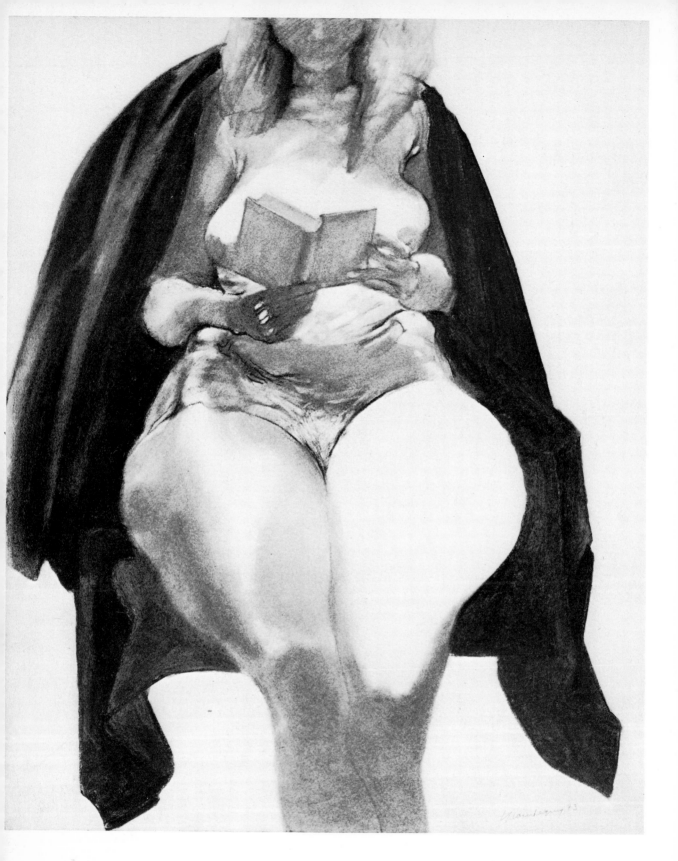

Jean Ipoustéguy 1920–

Woman Reading, in Black Cape 1973. Charcoal 69·3 x 55·8 cm (27 ¼ x 22 in)
Galerie Claude Bernard, Paris

The texture of the firm, rounded flesh is contrasted with the black cloak
enfolding the woman. Dense shading brings out the white enormity of the
thighs; and the small book, held in relatively tiny hands, transforms this
informally posed girl into a contemporary Venus of Willendorf.

Jean Ipoustéguy 1920–

Writing 1973. Charcoal and gouache 65·6 x 50·4 cm (25 ⅞ x 19 ⅞ in)
Galerie Claude Bernard, Paris

The figure of the girl writing is a study of what happens to the folds of the flesh
when the body is hunched over. A wealth of small, apparently extraneous forms
appears between breast and thigh.

Philip Pearlstein 1924–

Two Female Models on Chair and Rug 1975
wash 74·3 x 103·5 cm (29¼ x 40¾ in)
Courtesy of Allan Frumkin Gallery, Chicago

The reclining figure is seen in its totality, with strong foreshortening leading from
the head down the long expanse of the back to the heels. The pattern of the rug
sets off the smoothness of the flesh. The figure on the left, crouched on a chair
(which in its turn is also rendered in great detail), is cut off at the head and
elbow. The various parts of the body overlap: hand over breast, knee over
elbow.

   Every part of the composition, woman, chair or rug, is treated with equally
painstaking and polished attention to detail. The drawing is built up by the
rhythmic addition of details, some in harmony, others in brutal contrast.

Patrick Procktor 1936–

David and Mo V 1967
ink 40 x 50 cm (15¾ x 19⅝ in)
Redfern Gallery, London

This pen drawing reduces the bodies, one reclining, one sitting, and the bed, to their outlines. A feeling of form and three-dimensionality is nevertheless strongly conveyed. The figures and the bed are displayed in their entirety within the compass of the paper.

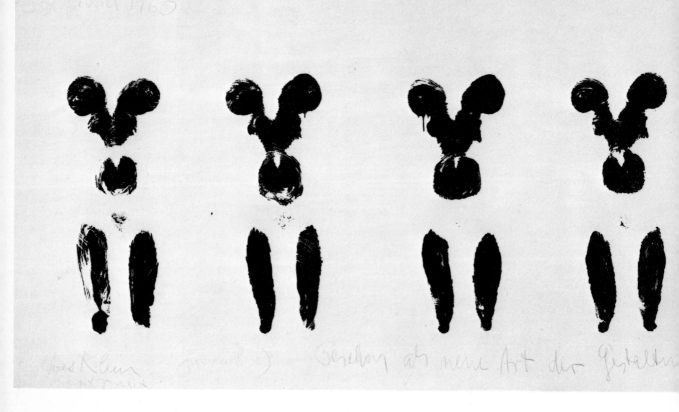

Yves Klein 1928–62

Celebration of a New Anthropometric Era 1960
Paint on canvas. Galerie Karl Flinker, Paris

These are the imprints left on a canvas by the body of a model which has been covered with blue paint by the artist. The surprising result is that a number of anatomical facts are thus directly conveyed; breasts, belly and thighs are clearly visible. The rest of the body can be reconstructed by the imagination of the viewer.

This near-mechanical transposition of a piece of nature into a two-dimensional element is of course a most extreme and individual piece of pictorial bravado.

Klein produced many of these artifacts in public, working sometimes with several models, giving the procedure a certain show-effect by the participation of musicians.

Jean Fautrier 1897–1964

Crouching Nude 1942. Ink 31·5 x 25 cm (12⅜ x 9⅞ in)
Collection Michel Couturier et Cie, Paris

The figure is reduced to a closed shape of convex lines of rhythmically varying intensity. This lends to the drawing a certain calligraphic quality, as much a written as a drawn statement, which is seen in the pressure of head, arms and trunk on the bent legs, which look almost like compressed springs.

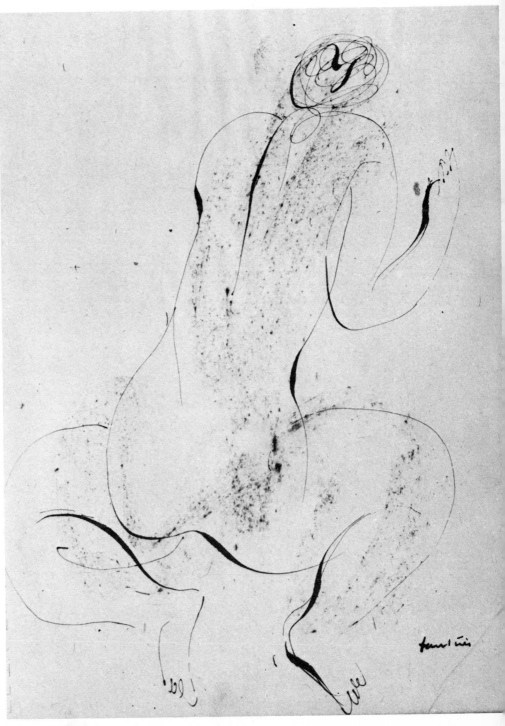

Claes Oldenburg 1929–

Seated Nude, Back View 1959
crayon 34·6 x 25·4 cm (13 ⅝ x 10 in)
Collection of the artist, New York

This spirited drawing of a woman sitting on a couch has something of a
shorthand jotting about it. The energetic swirling strokes of the crayon are
repeated in the background, small pictorial elements revolving around the
woman's back. The hair flowing down it adds a dark focal point.

Claes Oldenburg 1929–

Hanging Study, Giant Fan, Girl Demonstrating 1967. Pencil 101·6 x 66 cm (40 x 26 in)
Collection Elliott Abrams, New York

This large drawing introduces an element of Surrealism. The carefully observed
body displayed in a complicated acrobatic position is linked with a number of
accessories which lend themselves to more than one interpretation. The heavy
pencil is used with great verve, the quality of a sketchbook drawing being
transferred to a monumental format. A further Surrealist element, not strictly
visual, is brought in through the verbal allusion in the title.

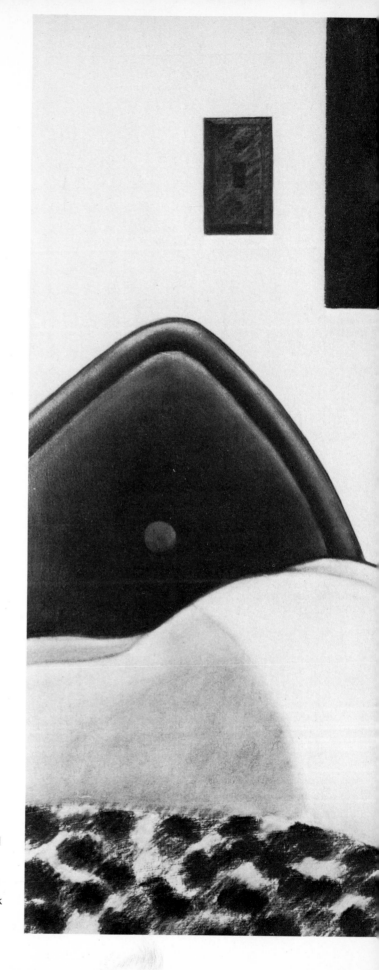

Tom Wesselmann 1931–

Drawing for G.A.N. 1961
charcoal on canvas 91·4 x 114·2 cm (36 x 45 in)
Collection Mr and Mrs B. Guttman, Brussels

In the studies for his cycle of paintings *The Great American Nude*, Wesselmann gives something more than mere graphic comments on the monumental sex-symbol that is his theme. For these large charcoal drawings display a surprising range of tonality, from the brittle darkness of the flowers and other objects surrounding the figure to the brilliant light patches of skin left by the bikini. Such contrasts of light and dark on the body, plus the provocative poses, are openly erotic and suggest a mass-produced intimacy.

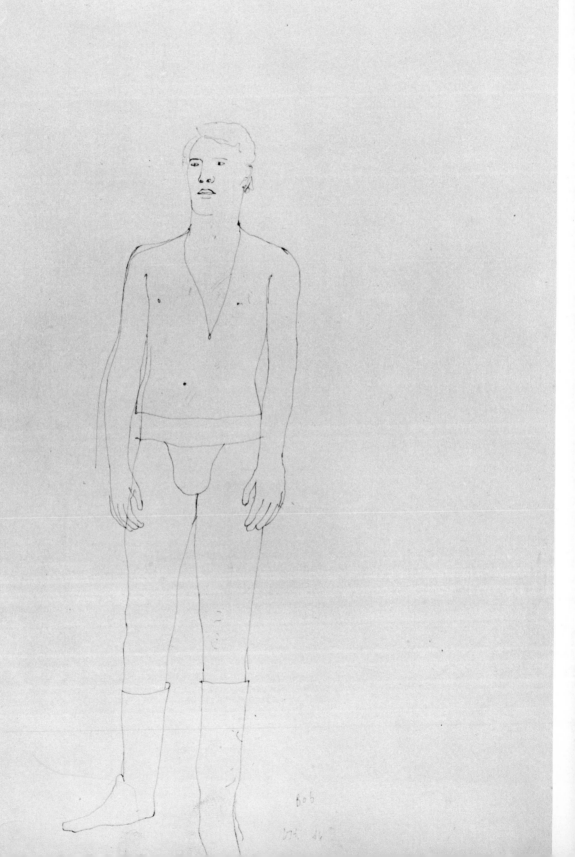

David Hockney 1937–

Two Boys 1961. Pencil 40·5 x 50·5 cm (16 x 19 ⅞ in)
Private collection

This refreshingly uninhibited drawing derives much from the contrast between
its utmost delicacy of line and shading and its subject matter, which is presented
with an unblinking directness. The movement of the reclining bodies is achieved
with economy and elegance; brisk tactile statements bring out the pattern of
the rug and the folds of the sheet.

David Hockney 1937–

Bob 1966. Ink 59 x 45·5 cm (23 ¼ x 17 ⅞ in)
Private collection

The straightforward linear pen-drawing contrasts the skin with various trappings
which stress the nakedness of the model.

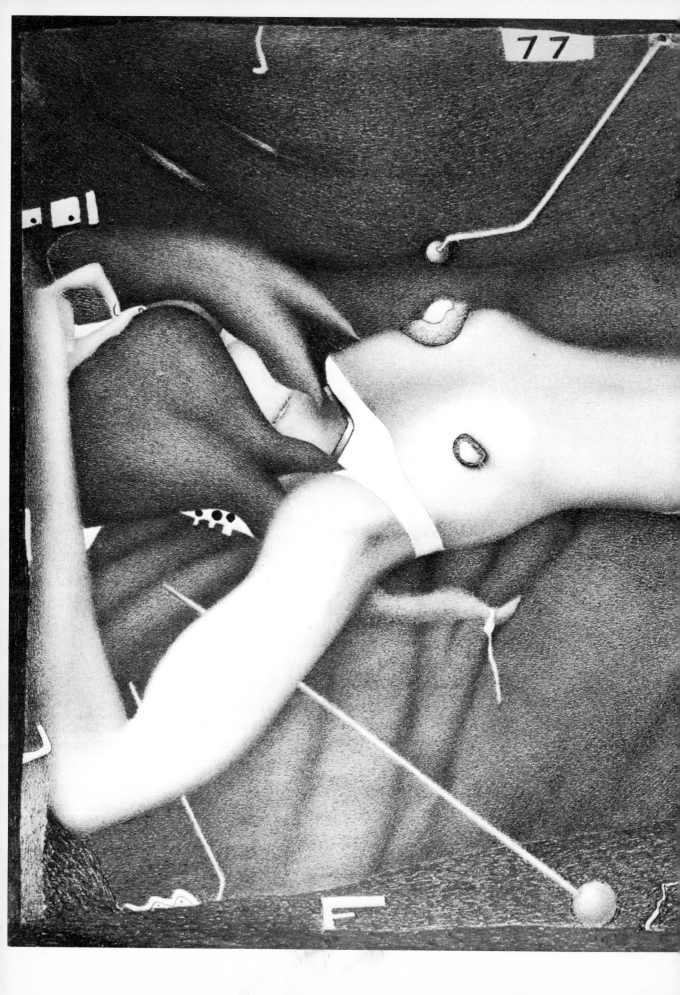

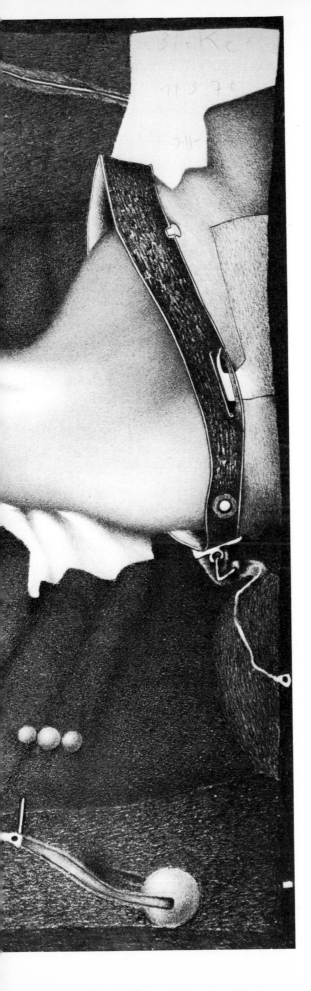

Horst Janssen 1929–

Birch Tree 1970

pencil and crayon 70 x 90 cm (27 ½ x 35 ⅜ in)
Galerie Brockstedt, Hamburg

The bizarre apparition emerges from the loosened belt.
Background and hair are laboriously shaded, leaving the
body in stark white contrast. There is much distortion: the
elongation of the trunk, the disproportionate enlargement of
the right arm, the fragment of grimacing face hidden behind
the hair. These exaggerated elements of flesh and vegetation
and mechanical details in the background conform, however,
to a highly individual logic of pictorial coherence.

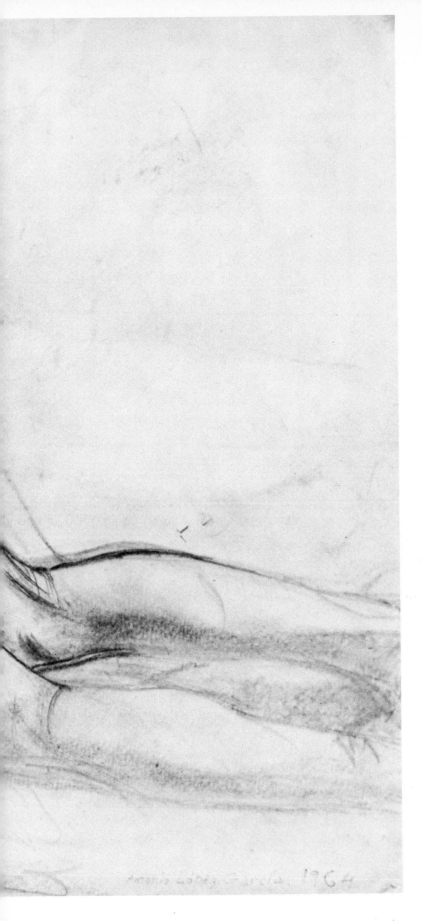

Antonio López García 1932–

Lovers 1964
pencil 23·5 x 32 cm (9 ¼ x 12 ⅝ in)
Collection Galerie Herbert Mayer-Ellinger,
Frankfurt am Main

The interlocked limbs of man and woman:
the act of love depicted in a cool and
seemingly detached manner. Only after a
second look does the metamorphosis of
visual curiosity and excitement into exact
observation and draughtsmanship become
apparent. The artist's sublimated naturalism
does not transform viewer into *voyeur*; there
is nothing embarrassing in this drawing.

Ernst Neizvestny 1926–

Seated Nude 1964. Flowmaster ink 44 x 31 cm (17⅜ x 12¼ in). Grosvenor Gallery, London

For this Soviet sculptor, the human body is relevant as a symbol of emotions, chiefly those of suffering and endurance. Having taken the basic proportions as a starting-point, Neizvestny systematically uses distortion to intensify expression, thereby creating an individual scheme of anatomical facts. His figures twist and turn, are elongated or foreshortened, yet never lose the forceful sense of organic cohesion.

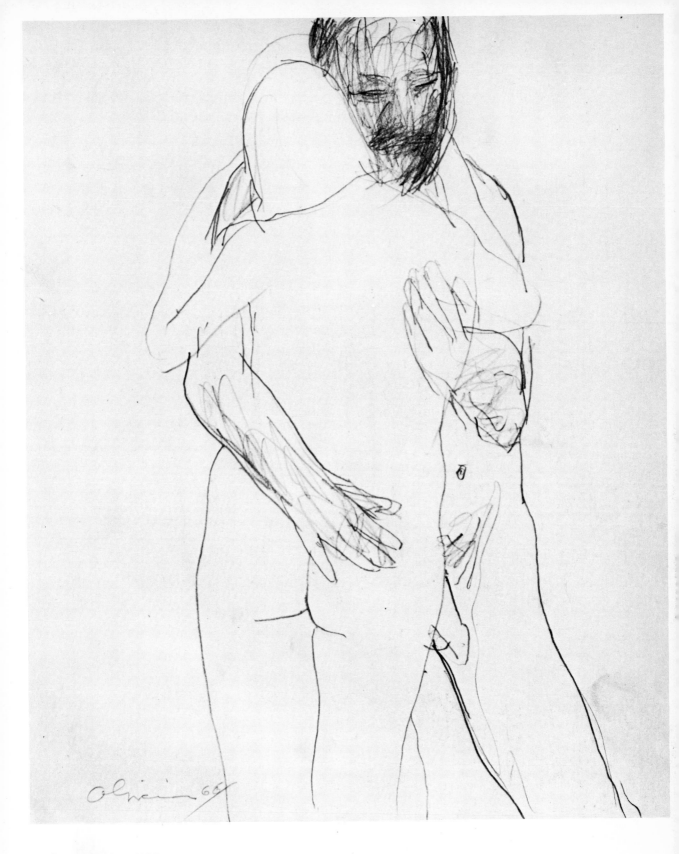

Nathan Oliveira 1928–

Couple 1966. Pencil 48·3 x 39·4 cm (19 x 15 ½ in). Collection of the artist

The woman is depicted by a continuous line. For the head of the man a loose
network of vertical strokes of the pencil creates a different texture and tone to
the smooth expanse of the woman's back.

   The tenderness of the couple's gesture is stated in the most direct and
straightforward way.

Allen Jones 1937–

Fit to Print 1974–5. Pencil 81·3 x 56 cm (32 x 22 in). Waddington Galleries, London

Drawings such as this by Allen Jones are not of nakedness but of various stages of 'un-dress'. Underwear, as a sort of second skin, accentuates the body instead of covering it. They are also closely observed slices of contemporary life, an ironic and fascinating comment on the mass-appeal of modern advertising.

Richard Lindner 1901–

Drawing for 'Miss American Indian' 1969–70. pencil on tracing-paper

Lindner's women wear their lingerie as an integral protective part of their anatomy, not unlike the armour of the rhinoceros. This gives their bodies an almost tactile, but hard and unyielding, surface. They are modern totems drawn with close affinity to nature, and if distortions occur, they always do so with a certain fetishist logic.

Acknowledgments

I would like to thank Erich Lessing for the photo sequence, C.N.P.Powell for much useful advice and for looking through my manuscript, E.J.Hobsbawm for helpful suggestions, Peter Vergo for reading the proofs, and my wife Alice for helping with the text.

I am also indebted to my artist colleagues and friends for many stimulating discussions on the subject of drawing, and to the Institute of European Studies in Vienna for the opportunity of putting some of my theories on the teaching of life-drawing to a practical test.

Many thanks also to the numerous public and private owners of works reproduced in this book.

Further reading

Bammes, Gottfried, *Die Gestalt des Menschen*, Dresden 1968.
Berger, John, *Ways of Seeing*, Harmondsworth and New York 1972.
Clark, Kenneth, *The Nude*, London and New York 1956.
Fischer, Ernst, *The Necessity of Art*, Harmondsworth and Baltimore 1963.
Gericke, Lothar, and Klaus Schöne, *Das Phänomen Farbe*, Berlin 1973.
Hiler, Hilaire, *The Painter's Pocket Book*, London and New York 1970.
Hofmann, Werner, *The Earthly Paradise*, New York 1961 and London 1965.
Hofstätter, Hans H., *Geschichte der Kunst und der künstlerischen Techniken*, Berlin 1965.

Photo credits

ACL, Brussels (Minne); Bulloz (Rouault *Nude*, Pascin, Matisse *Kneeling Nude*); Giraudon (Modigliani); Sidney Janis Gallery, New York (Segal, Oldenburg *Hanging Study*); Marlborough Fine Art, London (Schiele *Nude with Mauve Stockings*, Bacon); Galerie Herbert Mayer-Ellinger, Frankfurt am Main (Hockney, López García); Musées Nationaux, Paris (Bonnard, Léger *Male Nude*); Smith Anderson Gallery, San Francisco (Oliveira); Sotheby & Co., London (Kokoschka *Female Nude*, Delvaux); Walter Steinkopf (Ipoustéguy); Eileen Tweedy (Grant, John); James K. Ufford (Picasso *Bathers*); Rodney Wright-Watson (Neizvestny).